The
Tabaris Higł
Volunteers
September 1939

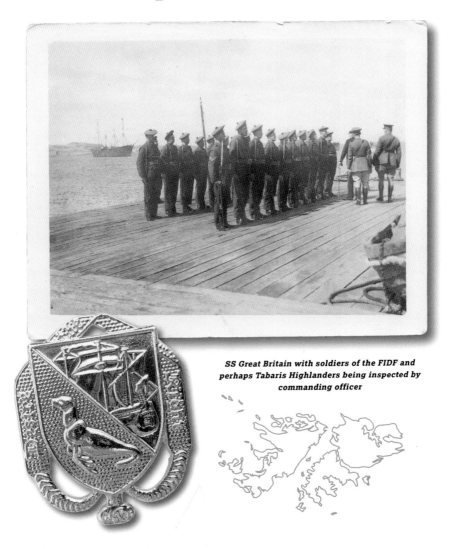

SS Great Britain with soldiers of the FIDF and perhaps Tabaris Highlanders being inspected by commanding officer

First published in the UK 2019

First Edition

Aileron Publishing

Printed and bound in the UK by Acanthus Press.

ISBN: 978 1 5272 4787 1

www.TabarisHighlanders1939.com

"THE TABARIS HIGHLANDERS"

1939

The 80th Anniversary

- 21st August 1939

  Admiral Graf Spee and Deutschland class cruisers with other surface raiders left Wilhelmshaven heading north up the Norwegian coast. Admiral Graf Spee travelled into the South Atlantic and Indian Ocean.

- August 1939

  Altmark with a cargo of Texan oil refuelled Admiral Graf Spee on 20th September 240 miles north of Ascension Island.

- 1st to 3rd September 1939

  World War 2 started, HMS Hotspur and HMS Havock left Freetown for Rio de Janeiro in the search for surface raiders.

- 4th September 1939

  Part of G Force.
  HMS Ajax – HMNZS Achilles intercepted Carl Fritzen and scuttled her and Olinda off Uruguay coast. Captain was then nicknamed, "One a day".

- 8th September 1939

  Admiral Graf Spee crossed Equator.

- 16th September 1939

  HMS Cumberland and HMS Havock left Rio de Janerio on escort duties.

- 26th September 1939

  Admiral Graf Spee released to follow orders. Over the next ten weeks she sank nine British ships. She could travel 16,300 nautical miles.

- Cricket Match

  The British Ambassador in Buenos Aires with SIS helped to enlist 33 to join the ship Lafonia for training in Port Stanley. German intelligence had knowledge of the deployment.

- 22nd September 1939

  Lafonia and small convoy left Montevideo at night.

- 27th September 1939

  Admiral Graf Spee split up with the Deutschland in the north Atlantic and the Graf Spee headed south under French flag passing the Azores accompanied by the Altmark.

3

- 27th September 1939

  The Tabaris Highlanders arrived in Port Stanley. Installation of: Gun Batteries/Signal Posts/sixteen coastal watching stations.

- October

  Governor Sir Herbert Henniken Heaton invited them to dinner. However, no one had a dinner jacket so the event was cancelled.

- 15th November 1939

  Admiral Graf Spee sank Africa Shell off Madagascar. Some codebooks were captured giving details on convoys, Admiral Graf Spee refuelled on 27th November 300 miles from Tristan Cunha.

- 5th December 1939

  The Abwehr commandeered the SS Ussukuma which was intercepted by HMS Ajax then scuttled off the Argentine coast. 107 crew were saved and interned in Simonstown, South Africa of which 82 were picked up by HMS Cumberland and then transferred to prison hulks in Falkland Islands.

- 8th December 1939

  Tabaris Highlanders and Corkie Robinson left Port Stanley on the SS Lafonia for Montevideo. Corkie Robinson stayed several days in a hotel overlooking Montevideo harbour.

- 13th December 1939

  Battle of the River Plate 150 miles from Uruguay.

- 14th December 1939

  The British tried to stop the Admiral Graf Spee sailing. This gave the British time to get more ships in case of a breakout.
  The Ambassador Sir Esmond Ovey in Argentina ordered 2,000 tons of fuel from Mar del Plata naval base. Captain Henry McCall Naval Attaché and Captain Max Miller SIS planned to give Germany the impression of a huge fleet gathering to destroy the pocket battleship all approved by Sir Eugen Millington-Drake.

Some of the 33 Tabaris Highlanders FIDF

Major John Morrough Commanding Officer previously of The Royal Irish Regiment

Ronald Campbell   Sergeant Group Commander

Thomas Dawson Sanderson   Corporal, President of Argentine Rugby Club

"Corkie" Charles Salkeld Robinson

Stiffy Rathbone (injured during the war)

Teddy Harrison

Perhaps were part of the 2nd group that embarked in 1940

Many other names are still to be found, so if you have any information that will help complete the list of names and any relevant information contact the website and author.

Twenty two applied to join the British Forces.

Picture of the whole group of Tabaris Highlander with their mascot.

The Falkland Islands in September 1939.

On 21st August 1939 a surface raider Admiral Graf Spee of the German Navy slipped out of Wilhelmshaven with the Admiral Scheer, a Deutschland class heavy cruiser. They headed north up the Norwegian coast and out into the Atlantic before war was declared. The Admiral Graf Spee met SS Altmark in the Azores on 28th August to refuel with Texan oil, replenishing the surface raider nine times during the mission with fuel and provisions away from the main shipping routes. She was also used as a floating POW camp.

In the early part of the war the Germans stuck to the Hague Convention, however, the Admiral Graf Spee passed the Azores flying the French Flag and with several other disguises (for example funnel and turret changes) to look like the Admiral Von Sheer or other ships. These were made up by the ships' carpenters to avoid detection so that they could get into position well in advance of the declaration of war and to confuse British intelligence.

View from Lafonia of Merchant ship and HMS Hotspur (H01)

During what has been called the phoney war several merchant ships may have been sent out months before to neutral ports and were waiting for orders to go operational. In the vast oceans a game of cat and mouse had started with the British preparing for the inevitable conflict.

British ships were refuelled at sea by ships like the Royal Fleet Auxiliary Olwen, Orangeleaf and Olynthus as the distances travelled were as much as 2,000 miles on every escort duty, keeping close to protect convoys up and down the coast of South America. Commodore Harwood adopted an odd days and even days escort north and south to reduce exposure to enemy attack and ensure efficient use of fuel.

Captain Hans Langsdorff was able to avoid contact with the Royal Navy for some time. His ship was nearly spotted when travelling south as the Admiral Graf Spee's seaplane an Ardo AR196 had flown within 30 miles quite close to HMS Cumberland which was travelling from Freetown to Rio De Janerio to join G Force under the command of Commodore Harwood but was not spotted. Later in the conflict the German seaplanes developed faults that hindered its reconnaissance and gunnery in the coming battle.

At this time "Corkie" Charles Salkeld Robinson was in Venezuela and Columbia after a short visit to Jamaica for his company Thomas Robinson of Rochdale. His work involved selling milling machinery.

Myrtle Bank Hotel, Kingston, Jamaica

Little did he know that he was to witness one of the most epic struggles against one of the most modern battleships afloat.

On the 3rd of August Corkie Robinson wrote to Mary Loraine-Smith; "It's a shame no spring stag hunting this year." Little did he know of the start of an aquatic hunt for a pocket battleship.

Preparing to leave early in the morning on the 4th of August he flew to Jamaica and then on to Lima stopping one night at Cristobel (Panama) and Guayaquil the port for Ecuador on the way to Caracas. The Venezuela government provided two chauffeurs to take him to potential milling sites. One chauffeur was familiar with the USA and the other a local saw nothing wrong with a straw mattress and cobwebs. Many places Corkie stayed in were local hotels very different to the grand hotels in the cities, quite often primitive. At one he counted one hundred flea bites, so took the necessary precautions on his second visit.

Grand Hotel Bolivar Lima, Peru

He sent a letter to his girlfriend almost everyday with news of his trip in great detail but never divulged any secrets. Their letters remained in a box for almost 60 years and shed light on his trip and thoughts on the gathering storm and the implications of getting home safe to join the RAF after his business trip.

After visiting Jamaica, Mexico, Venezuela and two months in the Falklands, he went back up the west coast of Chile to Ecuador and back to Jamaica, when his local agent almost died of pneumonia in Buenos Aires. In June 1940 he flew back to Buenos Aires before finally getting a berth on board ship to the United Kingdom. He was advised by the British Embassy in Buenos Aires that he was more use there than back in the UK until June 1940.

When the war started on the 3rd of September it was just hours later that HMS Ajax, stationed just off the coast of Uruguay sank a merchant ship called the Carl Fritzen and the Olinda on the 4th of September. The crew fondly called their captain on the Ajax, "one a day".

British Intelligence was very concerned of a potential plan to raid the Falklands and the whereabouts of many of the German ships was unknown. These included The SS Altmark, SS Tacoma, SS Dusseldorf, SS Nienburg, and SS Ussukuma.

On the outbreak of war several German ships scurried back to Germany and many were lost. The Monte Pascol, an ocean liner was in Argentinian waters and could have carried an invasion force from Patagonia to the Falklands.

SS Ussukuma

The Ussukuma was reported to be carrying wool but may have carried ammunition, explosives and torpedoes that would have been used to resupply U-boats and surface raiders. Her crew scuttled her as quickly as they could in full sight of HMS Ajax. All these ships were capable of raiding the Falklands and were either in the Pacific Ocean or the South Atlantic under Abwehr control. Some were lurking in neutral ports waiting for orders to rendezvous with surface raiders on set dates.

Corkie Robinson was heading down South America via Peru, Ecuador, and Venezuela where he crossed 15,000 ft. mountains in Bolivia and Chile. At one point in the Andes he visited hot springs that the Inca visited to cure their gout, keeping his girlfriend up to date on his trip south. His business trip covered vast distances to see clients of Thomas Robinson. He finally arrived in Buenos Aires, staying in an apartment with Neil Lamb, a friend who was working for Crossley Engineering. They had offices in Buenos Aires selling buses and other equipment to Argentina.

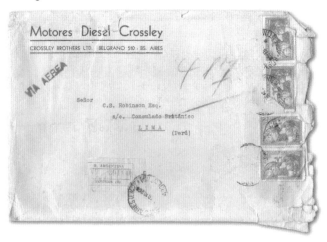

Shortly after his arrival Neil Lamb may have been in discussion we think with someone at the British Embassy. The British Ambassadors Sir Esmond Ovey in Argentina and Sir Eugen Millington Drake in Uruguay were trying to get a group of ex pats together to make up a party of volunteers to go to the Falklands. It seemed a good idea to invite several likely candidates to a cricket match as cover at the Hurlingham Club; this was a story I was told when I was about eight years old, this may have been my uncle putting a bit of spin on it. I remember it being a clandestine operation, twenty two plus the umpires might be sufficient. The timing and urgency of the deployment was critical, a more genteel gathering than the one held by the Germans at Luna Park.

In some of the pictures it is clear that some are still wearing cricket gear and the cricket pads went too. In contrast to the Nazi rally in Buenos Aires a year earlier this was a low key secret operation.

Blue Whale Arch

Christ Church Cathedral

There was a major concern that armed merchant ships with German militia were mustering in Patagonia Argentina for an attack on Port Stanley. There was tension in Argentina with the German ambassador Thermann whipping up support from the pro Nazi sympathisers in South America and Germany had in advance developed a network of agents across the continent. The Abwehr had commandeered ships and many thousands of Germans had gathered at a rally at Luna Park in Buenos Aires in 1938. There was bloodshed around the stadium and several deaths so British measures started to meet the threat after the sinking of ten merchant ships in 1939.

The Tabaris Highlanders (1939) as they were sometimes called were ready to deploy by the end of September. Some were partly recruited and some volunteered from the Anglo-Argentine community. They were named after the Tabaris nightclub, the most famous and notorious in South America.

Tabaris Nightclub

But in the case of my Uncle "Corkie" Charles Salkeld Robinson, he just happened to be there when the war started and he wanted to help.

Tabaris Highlander Corkie Robinson

On arrival in Port Stanley they were issued with similar hats to that of The Royal Regiment of Scotland. The Tam o' Shanter appears to be working headgear in all the pictures. There is no evidence of a cap badge so although the book has the crest of the FIDF on it, it is an informal association I have made in recognition of them enlisting and their commitment. In the picture on parade it seems likely they were issued with Lee Enfield rifles and were given basic training but some of the details are shrouded in mystery and time.

Tabaris Highlanders – FIDF with bayonets fixed

Corkie Robinson spent two months in the Falklands and would then witness the aftermath of one of the most important naval battles of the World War 2 before completing his business trip. He left South America on the Highland Patriot, who met her fate on a subsequent journey in October 1940.

Highland Patriot

Argentina had a large population with roots and ties with Germany and Britain so it was understandable that both combatants felt it necessary to think of new fronts that might be opened to gain a strategic advantage in this new war. The Abwehr German intelligence and its operatives would take the bait developed by the British to prevent the Admiral Graf Spee from leaving and perhaps making a dash for the Pacific and Japan. This was further hampered by the capture of the Dusseldorf by HMS Despatch in Chile on the 5th December.

Captain Hans Langsdorff had run out of options. Low on fuel and ammunition, fearing that it might end up in British hands with more naval ships arriving, Graf Spee was scuttled. Corkie Robinson saw the smouldering wreck as he played golf while staying at the Alvear Palace Hotel. During the early part of the war about two hundred Graf Spee's best trained sailors and some of the officers managed to get back to Germany while several hundred were interned in Argentina.

Hotel in Buenos Aires

On Wednesday 27th September Admiral Graf Spee and Admiral Sheer were let loose in the Atlantic Ocean, the same day that the Tabaris Highlanders arrived in Port Stanley. On November 15th Africa Shell was sunk near Madagascar and then the Admiral Graf Spee headed for the South Atlantic. The Tacoma, a German merchant ship, was also in the area resupplying and probably snooping on maritime shipping from the various ports up and down the South American coastline sending messages.

Prisoners from the sunken merchant ships were transferred to the Altmark but some of the officers had remained on board the Admiral Graf Spee.

The Royal Navy had also captured several hundred merchant seamen from merchant ships in the South Atlantic. These may have formed part of a raiding party had German plans worked. However, they were transferred to the hulks at Port Stanley and then sent to South Africa to be interned till the end of the war.

The Altmark's 299 prisoners were liberated in Norway's Jossingfjord after a raid by HMS Cossack on the 16th-17th February 1940 - quite an ordeal to be captive for six months for some of them.

"British Pirates" Germans upset by boarding party

In this picture of the destroyer it has had its number painted out and was an escort for the volunteers as they headed south from Montevideo.

Destroyer escort HMS Havock H43

On the 22nd of September HMS Hotspur escorted the first local convoy from Montevideo with HMS Havock after refuelling; escorting about four ships these included the Sussex, Roxby, El Ciervo and the Lafonia. With portholes blackened out and at dusk the convoy dispersed and HMS Hotspur escorted the Lafonia with the Tabaris Highlanders aboard to Port Stanley 1,066 nautical miles in approximately four and a half days.

23 Tabaris Highlanders on SS Lafonia

Some of the group look as if they had come straight from the cricket pavilion so there is perhaps some validity in Corkie's story he told me when I was very young.

During his stay on the island the Tabaris Highlanders FIDF may have installed several 4 inch guns and built observation posts across the islands.

Gun Emplacements on the Falklands

There are guns still at Gypsy Cove Yorke Bay, Cape Pembroke and Ordinance Point East Falkland. Perhaps others will come to light in future research. Some of these may have been installed by the Tabaris Highlanders and the FIDF.

Ship to transport 4" Vickers Naval Guns

Perhaps a Vickers 20 Pounder 4" Gun weighing 2,000KG and capable of firing 10,000 yards

Recruits either having gun drill or building a gun emplacement on the Falklands similar to that at Gypsy Cove. One picture shows the small ship used to transport the guns for the Tabaris Highlanders to install.

Hauling a 4" Vickers Gun into position

Remains of British 4" Mark 1V Naval Gun QF 4 - can be seen at
Gypsy Cove near Port Stanley, Falklands.

He also managed to do bit of rough shooting for geese and snipe but certainly not penguins. At that time the Falklands had five species of Penguin, King Penguins, Rockhopper, Gentoo and Magellanic and Macaroni.

A welcome change from Falkland Island mutton - something they had lots of at breakfast, lunch and supper.

On board the Lafonia they played shuffleboard on deck but on the islands were encouraged to play hockey and soccer. But the games often ended up as full blown rugby matches perhaps due to the corporal's love of that game.

Corporal Thomas Dawson Sanderson

Sergeant Ronald Campbell

Corkie Robinson was billeted at the Port Stanley Church Hall and received letters from his girlfriend, Mary Loraine-Smith. They later married on 18th February 1941 at St.Michael's Church, Stanton. At that time he was a junior flight officer in the Royal Air Force Volunteer Reserve.

Because of censorship Mary had no idea of what he was doing in the Falklands until he returned to Montevideo on the Lafonia.

In June 1939 HMS Exeter was in the West Indies and South American waters. Stationed in Bermuda, the crew found themselves destined for great things, as they were to represent the Royal Navy at the World's Fair in New York. Some of the crew of HMS Exeter's band played in Washington for the royal family. Some of the pictures show HMS Exeter at anchor in Port Stanley during October or November 1939.

HMS Exeter and Falkland Islands Flag.

After a short stay in Philadelphia and Baltimore HMS Exeter headed south to Miami and back to Bermuda. As war was declared Corkie Robinson was in Jamaica on his way to South America, Exeter was halfway between Freetown Sierra Leone and Rio de Janeiro where she had joined up with HMS Ajax who had just despatched the two German Merchant vessels Carl Fritzen and Olinda off the Uruguay coast on the 4th of September 1939.

British Cruiser in Falkland Sound between September to November 1939

In the First World War the Falklands was the scene of the destruction of Admiral Von Spee's fleet by Vice Admiral Doveton Sturdee. The area is strategic as a refuelling point for ships passing from the Pacific to the Atlantic Ocean, an ideal U Boat station, had the German Raiders captured the islands. In the aftermath of Pearl Harbour Churchill stationed 2,000 troops on the island.

Corkie Robinson had enjoyed several trips around South America. Sleeping in a railway carriage at the port of Arica he witnessed the arrival in March 1940 of some 250 German Jewish refugees en route to Bolivia. He continued his trip up the Chilean coast boarding the SS Orduna at San Antonio South of Valparaiso sometimes flying and sometimes on ships of The Pacific Steam Navigation Company, he must have seen lots of interesting places en route to Calloa.

Royal Naval Cruisers HMS Ajax or HMNZS Achilles in the Falklands

The next picture shows a smaller cruiser perhaps HMS Ajax. I have done some checks on its outline. It is possible that this could be HMNZS Achilles whose captain was W.E. Parry RN. HMS Ajax whose captain was F.S. Bell was involved in the destruction of several German merchant ships in September 1939.

Flying from Peru to Brazil and staying in The Esplanada Hotel Sao Paulo he also saw bullfighting in Rio de Janeiro.

*Who are you?! Corkie Robinson of the Tabaris Highlanders
(Falkland Islands Defence Force (FIDF)*

Had he slept in his suit for some time or was the turbulence crossing the Andes the cause of all the creases?

Always immaculately dressed, this was not his finest hour.

Six Tabaris Highlanders on The Falklands

Tabaris Highlanders in the Church Hall

There were so many developing theatres of war that the ingenuity and tenacity of these volunteers is something well worth recording and acknowledging as twenty two of them enlisted in the army, navy and RAF.

If the Admiral Graf Spee and U Boats had continued sinking ships we might not only have starved but we would never had heard of Fray Bentos, the name of a city in Uruguay close to the Argentina border 100 miles north of Buenos Aires. On one occasion a ship carrying 15,000 tons of beef was torpedoed. The Highland Patriot on each journey could carry 5.700 tons of refrigerated meat and other perishables vital for Britain's survival.

Leaving the River Plate and Buenos Aires

On deck playing Shuffleboard en route to Port Stanley on board the SS Lafonia.

SS Lafonia
Reproduced courtesy of the
Falkland Islands Government / www.falklandstamps.com

℟℟

Alvear Palace Hotel
Buenos Aires

My darling Mene,

I still have no letter from you since I returned to B.A. so I expect you must have sent them to the Falklands or else they have got lost or delayed. I have been very busy this week getting my passport etc fixed up for my trip to Chile & Peru. I am going to leave here on Sunday by train & go to Mendoza which is on the Argentine side of the Andes. Then I am going to meet our agent & we are going to drive over the Andes by car. It should be a very interesting trip according to the people whom I have talked to & who have done the journey already. Apart from this the week has been most uneventful except that the heat has continued until the last two days, & as a result I have been going out to Hurlingham (the country Club) whenever possible & spent all the week end there in the bathing pool.

Fortunately Neil Lamb, with whom I used to share a flat when I was in B.A. before going to the Falklands, has a car & as we are now living together in the same hotel I go out with him a lot to Hurlingham both in the evenings & at the week ends. It really would be most unpleasant if I could not do this as the only other means of getting out there is by train which takes about an hour. The other evening when I was out with Neil having coffee & drinks in a bar an German officer came in off the "Graf Spee". He spoke English fairly well & we had quite a long talk with him in the hopes of getting a little information. Unfortunately without success.

DOS DE ESTAS HOJAS Y UN SOBRE DE VÍA AEREA PESAN 5 GRAMOS

Tabaris Club

Corkie Robinson in a well-tailored suit holding an umbrella with friends outside a club in Buenos Aires perhaps the Tabaris, the name used by the volunteers. He spent several weeks criss-crossing South America before and after the main events crossing the Andes to meet Chilean clients and back to a leaving party before joining them on the Highland Patriot for the voyage home.

On his return to Buenos Aires on the 8th December just days before the Battle of the River Plate he stayed at the Hotel Alvear Palace Hotel. While playing golf he looked out to sea at wreck of the Admiral Graf Spee sticking out of the water belching smoke four days after it was scuttled.

The funerals of some German sailors took place in Montevideo. There followed a chance encounter meeting between an officer of the Graf Spee and Corkie Robinson at a hotel where Corkie and his friend tried to extract information about the ship and what was happening. The German officer said, "If Hitler does not make a mistake he will win the war". Pressed if he was a Nazi the German officer declined to comment.

Corkie organised a cocktail party for the Tabaris Highlanders to say farewell before leaving for the next leg of his business tour.

The day after the battle he had seen the battleship in the harbour in Montevideo from his hotel bedroom. Once the danger of attack from Germany became less of a threat the volunteers were prepared to go back to work or join up in various arms of the services, many returning on the RMS Highland Patriot.

On 25th November 1940 he became a Pilot Officer on RAFVR as he had some flying experience and was stationed in Newton Stewart Scotland.

Flight Officer C S Robinson RAFVR

When I was about eight years old Uncle Corkie told me that he had been asked by a German midshipman to send a message to Wilhelmshaven for his wife who was expecting a baby to say he had survived the attack on the Admiral Graf Spee.

I remembered this story as I rummaged through a box of old photographs several years after Corkie Robinson's death. Together with his letters I have assembled his story with the pictures of the contingent which I believe is probably the only photographic record which includes penguins! I hope to gather more details of the others who served with him before publication or after as his story unfolds.

It occurred to me that this story may never have been completely documented or the bravery and commitment each of these men made to their country and friends. Had there been an attack it would have had a very different outcome. It probably all started as bit of an adventure for him but the seriousness of these events were to rapidly unfold with the loss of about seventy Royal Naval sailors at The Battle of The River Plate.

A group of 25 Tabaris Highlanders FIDF in Port Stanley 1939
with their mascot a small dog in the front row.

Corkie Robinson and the others were given basic training and toughened up as one can see from the pictures he took at the time which give lots of detail on what they did.

Naval assets on the move with two regulars of the FIDF

The nesting of the penguins is also an indication of the time of these events. I was not certain which month he arrived in the Falklands with his group but it seems likely late September 1939. Further research on nesting penguins led to another clue to Corkie's whereabouts. The photograph of whalebones outside Port Stanley's Christ Church Cathedral provided an additional clue. Many years later my cousin and I took Uncle Corkie and Aunt Mary to see the SS Great Britain in Bristol for a second encounter much to the horror of Corkie who was not impressed with its new livery.

He was probably quite happy knowing how it was back in 1939 when he did basic military training helping to prepare shore defences and military installations.

The picture shows Falkland Island Defence Force on parade

The picture show soldiers in full uniform on parade with the senior officers inspecting them, also two pictures show a group with Tam o' Shanter hats being inspected.

Lafonia's Destroyer Escort HMS Hotspur H01

Just days before the Battle of the River Plate another German Merchant ship the SS Ussukuma commandeered by the Abwehr was sunk on 5th December off the Argentine coast with 107 crew saved who were then destined to be interned in South Africa.

On the 12th December an Enigma Message sent to Admiral Graf Spee was received and is perhaps of interest to those who follow the activities of Bletchley Park. It indicated that the merchant ship Africa Star was heading south from Tenerife to Buenos Aires another ideal opportunity for the Graf Spee, at the same time Commodore Henry Harwood was heading north to intercept the pocket battleship on its projected course with HMS Ajax and HMNZS Achilles and at the same time using the two destroyers and HMS Cumberland for extra cover.

With work completed, Corkie Robinson left Port Stanley on board the SS Lafonia on about the 5th of December for Montevideo. The British squadron was steaming north in search of the German Raider Graf Spee.

British Intelligence was active in these parts headed up by Captain Max Miller and Captain H.W.U. McCall. Aware of the sympathetic leanings of some Germans in Argentina during the 2nd World War, information from a Dutch merchant ship about the whereabouts of the SS Ussukuma helped seal the fate of both ships within ten days.

The Exeter left Freetown at the start of the war and was later refuelling in Rio de Janerio next to a German merchant ship alongside that gave them "Three Cheers"- but they would not have done so if they had been at sea. As the dawn broke on the 13th of December the gloves were off. It is possible that with Bletchley Park code breaking, messages sent to the Graf Spee about a merchant ship would compromise Captain Hans Langsdorff's position.

HMS Ajax, HMNZS Achilles and HMS Exeter were on watch looking for a Raider and Commodore Harwood plotted the position of each ship sunk and speculated that a pocket battleship would be at the mouth of The River Plate on Friday 13th December 1939 and indeed there was. I was having a chat with someone in the navy who told me that the Morse Code operators developed a style of sending messages and it was possible to detect the characteristics and plot the position of various ships even as early as 1939 by checking the style of the operators.

British intelligence SIS and their operatives in Buenos Aires Henry McCall the Military attaché and Captain Rex Miller were active in keeping a watchful eye on German activity. At this time the navy probably was stretched globally so the Falklands was not a priority until it was aware of the huge losses in shipping just one ship could inflict. Many of the sailors that were rescued after their sinking were transferred to the German ship Altmark and some to the Graf Spee.

During the battle HMS Exeter lost 61, HMS Ajax 7 and HMNZS Achilles 4. Many were buried at sea and on the way to the Falklands, several more died and were buried on the island, while others were nursed at the local hospital. Some of the less injured stayed with local families while the crew repaired weakened bulkheads ready for the journey home.

The King Edward V11 Memorial Hospital looked after some of the casualties in Port Stanley.

Reproduced courtesy of the
Falkland Islands Government / www.falklandstamps.com

HMS Exeter arrived in the Falklands for extensive repairs. Helped by the SS Lafonia they transported metal plates and welding rods plus urgently needed medical staff and supplies for the injured in Port Stanley hospital. After repairs HMS Exeter went back to Plymouth Britain in great triumph where the crew were met by First Sea Lord Winston Churchill, for lunch at the Exeter Guildhall.

In his letter dated 22nd June 1940, written on board the Highland Patriot he and many of the Tabaris Highlanders and others were eager to return home to join up. The guns on the ship were checked by the Marines, some were given drill by the Royal Marine sergeant, concerned about how many submarines might be following them, as on its trip south from Greenock via the Canaries it was attacked by a French submarine Fresnel Q-143 on the 29th December 1939 it fired back forcing the French submarine to retire so it is clear nobody was taking any chances on the long trip home.

Concerns were raised by Corkie and he was lucky to have got home unscathed as on a subsequent trip The Highland Patriot was torpedoed and sunk by U38 commanded by Heinrich Liebe on the 1st October 1940 with 3 dead and 169 survivors, 500 miles west of Bishops Rock, the survivors were picked up by HMS Wellington (L65) now berthed in the Thames at Whitehall.

HMS Wellington

The Highland Patriot sailed from Buenos Aires to Montevideo where everyone met for a leaving party at The English Club. After a game of golf Corkie saw the remains of the Admiral Graf Spee for the last time, sticking out of the water on the skyline. He then sailed up the coast to Santos in Brazil staying a couple of days in Sao Paulo.

The Admiral Graf Spee was scuttled away from the main shipping route in neutral Uruguay. At the time Corkie Robinson knew that Thomas W Ward Ltd had managed to acquire the wreck via an intermediary. A double agent Julio Vega-Helguara had bought the wreck in February 1940 for about £14,000. The British government was determined to find out about its Radar Directional Finder (RDF) on board and the frequency or wavelength.

In my research I also found out that a Royal Naval torpedo officer and diver Lt. Guy P. Kilroy dived on the wreck to find out more about her design and details for the admiralty in particular the welded hull. With others in the team Mr Labouchere Bainbridge-Bell was flown by Sunderland flying boat part of the way to avoid suspicion and other experts joined for several weeks work removing guns and parts to ship back to the UK for technical analysis.

With thanks to my "Uncle Corkie" for all he did for his country, friends and family and in particular his contribution to my education through a charitable trust set up in 1967.

The Editor

The author's meticulous research provides an engaging account of his uncle Corkie's role as a volunteer in the FIDF, aka The Tabaris Highlanders.

Charles Salkeld Robinson - was one of a group of young men, far from home who unhesitatingly and willingly stepped up to do their bit to stop the Nazis in the theatre of the South Atlantic. The author tells his story with fondness, a tribute to the memory of his uncle and his chums who helped in the defence of the Falkland Islands at the onset of WWII.

Mary Mc Veigh

Tabaris Highlanders' mascot

Governor & Corporal

Tabaris Highlanders on board Lafonia